—

CURLING

Annalise Bekkering

WEIGL PUBLISHERS INC.

Published by Weigl Publishers Inc.
350 5th Avenue, Suite 3304, PMB 6G
New York, NY 10118-0069

Copyright © 2007 Weigl Publishers Inc.
www.weigl.com

Library of Congress Cataloging-in-Publication Data

Bekkering, Annalise.
   For the love of curling / Annalise Bekkering.
   p. cm. — (For the love of sports)
   Includes index.
   ISBN 1-59036-402-3 (hard cover : alk. paper) —
   ISBN 1-59036-403-1 (soft cover : alk. paper)
  1. Curling—History.   I. Title. II. Series.
  GV845.B45 2007   796.964—dc22   2005026968

Printed in the United States of America

1 2 3 4 5 6 7 8 9 10 09 08 07 06

Cover: Cassie Johnson of the United States prepares
to deliver a rock during the World Women's Curling
Championship final between the United States and
Sweden on March 27, 2005 in Glasgow, Scotland.
Her team won the silver medal.

Photograph Credits
United States Curling Association: pages 16L and 17R;
Andrew Kalver and courtesy of Scott Paper Limited:
page 19L.

Editor
Frances Purslow

Design and Layout
Terry Paulhus

All of the Internet URLs
given in the book were valid
at the time of publication.
However, due to the
dynamic nature of the
Internet, some addresses
may have changed, or sites
may have ceased to exist
since publication. While
the author and publisher
regret any inconvenience
this may cause readers, no
responsibility for any such
changes can be accepted
by either the author or
the publisher.

Every reasonable effort
has been made to trace
ownership and to obtain
permission to reprint
copyright material.
The publishers would be
pleased to have any errors
or omissions brought to
their attention so that
they may be corrected
in subsequent printings.

Contents

All about Curling

Curling is a winter sport that is played on long sheets of ice. Players slide large stones down the ice. They aim for the center of a circular target at the other end. The team with the rock or rocks closest to the center scores points.

Curling has been nicknamed "the roaring game" because of the sound the rock makes as it slides along the ice.

No one knows exactly when and where curling began. One very cold day, a man likely picked up a rock from the ground and threw it down an icy stream. Others saw what he was doing and joined him. Some people believe curling was first played in Germany or the Netherlands. The earliest proof of the sport was found in Scotland, dating back to the 1500s. Small, flat stones called "loofies" have been found in dried-up ponds in Scotland. The oldest known stone is marked with 1511. Old curling stones were also made out of cannonballs, wood, and frozen dirt.

By 1739, curling rules were made. Players were not allowed to swear or gamble during matches. In 1790, John Carnie made the first **artificial** curling rink in Scotland. He sprayed water on pavement until it froze. In 1828, he made a clay pond that was used as a curling rink.

The first curling club in the United States was the Orchard Lake Curling Club. It was organized in 1832 by some Scottish men who had moved to Detroit. Over time, curling gained popularity. Today, more than 20,000 people curl in the United States. There are more than 100 rinks across the country.

Today curling is enjoyed by people of all ages in more than 30 countries.

CHECK IT OUT

To learn more about the history of curling, go to **www.hickoksports.com** Then click on History, and then Index by Sport.

Getting Started

Curlers slide heavy stones down sheets of ice. After a stone is thrown, two teammates slide along with the stone and sweep the ice in front with a broom. The sweeping melts a thin layer of ice, speeding up the rock and keeping it on a straight path.

Curlers wear loose, comfortable clothing so they can move easily. Members of curling teams often wear matching pants and jackets.

Curling rocks are made in Scotland. The granite used to make the rocks is **quarried** in Wales or Scotland. Each one weighs between 42 and 44 pounds (19 and 20 kilograms). There are special stones for children. They are smaller and weigh 25 pounds (11 kg). These rocks are easier for young children to slide down the ice.

Each team has eight color-coded rocks. There is a plastic handle on top of each stone for a curler to hold when throwing the rock. There is an indent in the bottom of the rock, so only part of the stone touches the ice.

Early brooms were made of stiff corn fibers. Today, brush heads are made of nylon, hog hair, or horsehair.

Curlers wear a slider on one of their shoes. A slider helps a curler glide along with a stone while they are sweeping. The other shoe has a gripper to help prevent the curler from falling.

The Curling Ice

Curling ice is colder than hockey ice. This makes it harder and less likely to dent from the stones. If there is a dent or bump in curling ice, it can send the stone off course. Before every match, an **ice technician** sprays the ice with tiny droplets of water. The droplets freeze onto the surface, forming small, bumpy **pebbles**. The rock rides across the top of these pebbles. Very little of the rock comes into contact with the ice.

Curlers use their brooms for balance as they deliver their rocks.

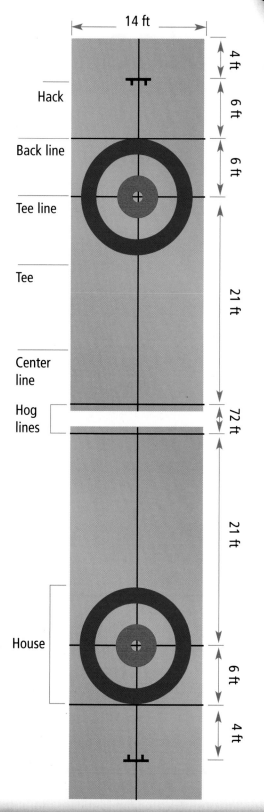

14 ft

Hack

Back line

Tee line

Tee

Center line

Hog lines

House

4 ft

6 ft

6 ft

21 ft

72 ft

21 ft

6 ft

4 ft

Curlers play on a sheet of ice that is 146 feet (44.5 meters) long and 14 feet (4.3 m) wide. There is a target, called a house, at either end of the ice. The house consists of three colored circles. The tee is a small hole in the center of the house. The team with the rock closest to the tee wins points for that **end**. It receives one point for every stone it has in the house that is closer than the opposite team's stones.

A **hack** is frozen in the ice 4 feet (1.2 m) from each end of the ice sheet. A curler puts one foot in the hack and pushes off. The curler glides with the stone, and must release the rock before passing the nearest **hog line**. The rock must travel farther than the hog line on the other end of the ice, but must not pass the back line. If the rock does not pass the hog line, it is removed from the game. If the rock passes through the house to the back line, it is also removed from the game.

Rules of Curling

A curling match is divided into 10 ends. During each end, players on both teams take turns throwing two rocks each down the sheet of ice toward the house. When the end is over, the rocks are scored, then moved to the side. Then the teams begin the next end throwing rocks in the opposite direction. A coin toss at the beginning of the game decides which team gets the **hammer**. The winner of the coin toss throws the last rock in the first end. If the team throws its last rock closest to the tee, it wins points in that end.

In this end, the yellow team receives a single point because there is one yellow stone closer to the tee than any red stones. The red team gains no points.

CHECK IT OUT

Learn more about curling rules at

www.curlingschool.com

W hen a player throws a rock down the ice, two sweepers from his or her team slide down the ice. They sweep ahead of the rock to speed it up and keep it sliding in a straight line. When a rock slows down, it begins to **curl**. Sweepers are not allowed to touch the rock.

When each end is finished, a team is awarded points for the rocks it has closer to the tee than any of the other team's rocks. Sometimes a long rod called a measure is used to determine whose rock is closer to the tee. Stones must be in the house to be counted. The team that scored points throws the first rock in the next end. If the score is tied when the game finishes, the teams play an extra end.

The measuring rod is 6 feet (1.8 m) long. It is used only after the last stone of the end has come to a stop.

Rink Positions

A curling team is also called a rink. There are four positions in a curling rink, each with different skills. Each of the four members of a team throws two rocks. They alternate with the other team. Players also sweep the rocks of their teammates.

The leader of the team is called the skip. He or she decides the team's strategy and directs the other players as to where to place their stones. The skip also throws the last two stones in each end, so he or she must be able to make shots under pressure. How well the last two stones are thrown often determines the outcome of the game. The skip holds the broom as a target for the other players. He or she tells them how hard to throw the rocks and which way to curl them. Sweepers listen for the skip to say when to begin sweeping. The skip must be able to **read the ice** in order to know how the rock will behave and to set up the target properly.

The only player who does not take a turn sweeping is the skip.

The third is a good shot-maker and sweeper. He or she works with the skip to decide the team's strategy. The third is sometimes called the vice-skip. The third throws soft weight hits, lightly tapping stones into different positions. He or she also throws **takeout shots**. When it is the skip's turn to throw, the third stands in the house holding the broom, to help the skip aim. The thirds on each team also keep score.

Sweepers must be able to judge how fast a rock is moving and when they should sweep.

The second throws rocks after the lead. He or she throws rocks hard and precisely, to remove the other team's rocks. The second must also place rocks exactly where the skip wants them, in order to score points.

The lead is the first person to throw stones down the ice. The lead often places rocks at the front of the house as guards. The other players on the team then try to curl their rocks in behind the guards.

CHECK IT OUT

To try virtual curling, go to **www.toktaki.com/free-games/** *Then select Virtual Curling.*

Where the Action Is

ocal curling rinks give curlers of all ages and skill levels the chance to play. Curling rinks have different leagues to join. They also have **bonspiels** to compete in. There are many different levels of competition. Many curlers enter bonspiels to win prizes and money.

Although curling began as an outdoor sport played on frozen lakes and ponds, most games today are played indoors at curling clubs or ice rinks.

Bonspiels are held all over the world. Countries send their best curling teams to compete against each other at the World Championships and the Olympic Winter Games.

The World Curling Championships are held every year. This bonspiel is attended by the 10 best curling teams from around the world. The U.S. men's team has been champions four times. In 1965, U.S. skip Bud Somerville became the first non-Canadian to win the tournament. The U.S. women's team won the championship in 2003.

The Ogden Ice Sheet was the site of the curling events for the 2002 Salt Lake City Winter Olympics.

The best curling teams in the world compete in the Winter Olympics. Curling became an official Olympic sport in 1998, in Nagano, Japan. That year, the Swiss men's curling team won the gold medal. The first women's team to win gold in the Olympics was Canada. Before that, curling was an exhibition sport in the Olympics.

Pioneers of the Sport

Millions of people worldwide play this winter sport. Others have enjoyed watching these curling stars at the rinks or on television.

RAYMOND "BUD" SOMERVILLE

POSITION
Skip
HOMETOWN
Superior, Wisconsin

Career Facts:

- Bud was Wisconsin State Champion 14 times.
- He has won the Men's U.S. National Championship five times.
- Bud won the bronze medal at the 1992 Winter Olympics and placed fourth in 1988.
- He was the first non-Canadian to win the World Championship in 1965 and won again in 1974.
- Bud was the first inductee into the U.S. Curling Hall of Fame.

SANDRA SCHMIRLER

POSITION:
Skip
HOMETOWN:
Biggar, Saskatchewan

Career Facts:

- Sandra's rink won the first official gold medal for curling at the 1998 Olympic Winter Games in Nagano, Japan.
- She won the Canadian Championships in 1993, 1994, and 1997.
- In 2000, Sandra was awarded the Saskatchewan Order of Merit for her accomplishments.
- After Sandra passed away in 2000 due to cancer, the Sandra Schmirler Foundation was set up to help families of sick children.

COLLEEN JONES

POSITION:
Skip
HOMETOWN:
Halifax, Nova Scotia

Career Facts:

- Colleen has won 14 Nova Scotia women's titles.
- She holds the most National Championships in Canadian history.
- Colleen won the Scott Tournament of Hearts in 1982, 1999, 2001, 2002, and 2003.
- Her rink won gold in the 2001 World Championships and silver in 2003.

ED LUKOWICH

POSITION:
Skip
HOMETOWN:
Calgary, Alberta

Career Facts:

- Ed's rink won the World Championships in 1986.
- He won the bronze medal for curling at the Olympic Winter Games in 1988.
- Ed represented Alberta at five Brier Championships and was the champion in 1978 and 1986.
- He has written many books about curling, including *The Joy of Curling* and *Curling to Win*.

Superstars of the Game

Today's curling heroes dazzle audiences with their accuracy and strategy in international events.

PETE FENSON

POSITION
Skip
HOMETOWN
Bemidji, Minnesota

Career Facts:

- Pete was U.S. National Men's Champion in 1993, 1994, and 2003.
- His rink qualified for the 2006 Olympic Winter Games.
- Pete was named United States Curling Association Athlete of the Year in 2003 and 2005.
- He was Minnesota State Men's Champion five times in his career.

CASSANDRA JOHNSON

POSITION
Skip
HOMETOWN
Bemidji, Minnesota

Career Facts:

- Cassandra won the silver medal at the 2005 World Curling Championships.
- Her rink qualified for the 2006 Winter Olympics.
- Cassandra won gold at the 2002 Junior Worlds and silver in 2003.

RUSS HOWARD

POSITION:
Skip
HOMETOWN:
Midland, Ontario

Career Facts:

- Russ has played on the provincial rinks for Ontario and New Brunswick.
- His rink won the World Curling Championships in 1987 and 1993.
- *Sweep Magazine* named Russ the Curler of the Century.
- He has been a skip at the Brier 13 times, which is a record.

JENNIFER JONES

POSITION:
Skip
HOMETOWN:
Winnipeg, Manitoba

Career Facts:

- Jennifer was the 2005 Scott Tournament of Hearts Canadian Champion.
- She participated in the Scott Tournament of Hearts provincial championships each year from 1997 to 2003.
- Jennifer was the 1995 Canadian Junior Bronze Medalist.
- She was also the 1994 Canadian Junior Champion.

Staying Healthy

To stay in shape, athletes need to drink plenty of water. Even though curling is not overly tiring, curlers still sweat. Curlers drink water throughout the game to nourish their muscles.

Healthy food choices are also important. Before a match, curlers should eat carbohydrates, such as pasta or rice, to provide energy. During a game, eating fruit will give athletes an extra energy boost. Protein helps build muscle, and milk products make strong bones. A balanced diet containing all of these food groups will increase a curler's performance.

All athletes, including curlers, need to maintain a good diet in order to perform their best.

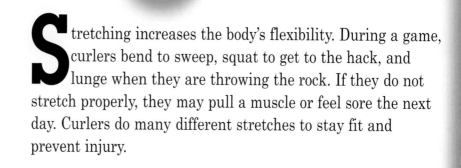

Stretching increases the body's flexibility. During a game, curlers bend to sweep, squat to get to the hack, and lunge when they are throwing the rock. If they do not stretch properly, they may pull a muscle or feel sore the next day. Curlers do many different stretches to stay fit and prevent injury.

To stretch their legs, curlers do lunge stretches. They stretch their left leg out behind them and keep their right knee over their right foot. Placing their hands on the floor on either side of their right foot, they press their hips toward the floor. They hold this position for 20 seconds. Then they switch legs.

To stay injury-free, curlers stretch their muscles before and after games.

Curling Brain Teasers

Test your curling knowledge by answering these brain teasers!

Q Name the positions on a curling team.

A They are lead, second, third, and skip.

Q Who was the first American skip to win the World Curling Championship?

A Raymond "Bud" Somerville won in 1965, and again in 1974.

Q In what ways is curling ice different from hockey ice?

A Curling ice is colder and harder than hockey ice. It is covered in tiny bumps called pebbles, which help the stones travel down the ice.

Q Where was the first artificial curling rink made?

A It was made in Scotland in 1790.

Q What are curling brush heads made of?

A Brush heads are made out of hog hair, horse hair, or nylon.

Q Why do curlers sweep in front of a rock?

A Sweeping causes the ice to melt. This makes the rock travel faster and straighter.

Glossary

artificial: man-made

bonspiels: curling tournaments

curl: travel in a curve

end: a part of the match where each player throws two stones

hack: a foothold that players push off from when delivering the rock

hammer: the last rock of an end

hog line: a line marked on either end of the ice sheet in front of the house. Players must not pass it when throwing a rock, and the rock must reach the hog line on the other end of the ice.

ice technician: someone who prepares the curling ice before a game

pebbles: small bumps on the surface of the ice that help the rocks travel quickly

quarried: cut or dug a type of stone or rock from the ground

read the ice: notice the ice conditions and consider how the rocks will be affected by them

takeout shots: hard shots that remove the other teams' rocks

Index